Please don't trample us; we are trying to grow!

Steph Morris

Fair Acre Press

First published in Great Britain in November 2020 by Fair Acre Press

www.fairacrepress.co.uk

A CIP catalogue record for this book is available from the British Library

ISBN 978-1-911048-44-2

Typeset by Nadia Kingsley

Cover image © Steph Morris 2020

For Tom

Contents

On arrival

I'll rock up one day
to a do like this
dead, perfect
on-my-way-here
anecdote: car cut me up
on the Old Cunt Road,
knocked me sideways flat,
bike bashed bent,
worse than me, to see,
saved, sprayed white,
locked to railings where
friends then left flowers,
fluffy toys, and poems,
my family deciding
to scatter my ashes
round roses, white
tinged red, here
each year after,
crying at the good
the potash would do.
Unlike my poor bike,
I kept my shape.
Last thing I remember,
the driver defensive
as I gazed along ground
you shouldn't lie on, grey,
grim, at my yellow bag,
reached a raw arm in
to note the numberplate,
inches from my face,
cross about the time
I'd waste in hospital,

worrying who would do
my work. Deciding
it was worse: who
would bin my things.
After that I couldn't see,
or hear, a relief from
shouting and sirens,
and, well, here I am.

What to take on flight

Chloe, not your platforms. Put your trainers on. No, don't put the platforms in your bag. No! We can only take one pair of shoes each. And not that bag, the rucksack. I don't care if it doesn't go with your jacket. It's an Ortlieb, it's stronger. I may need you to carry Archie, darling. All that netball. You'll be fine. Yes your phone's a good idea. And the charger. Well we don't know where it will work and when but... Chloe obviously it would be nice to drive but Daddy has checked. He's been listening to the radio, watching the news – well there is only news – and the net. The queues are too long. It'd be dangerous stranded in a car. This way we get out quicker. Sweetie there is no chance of getting on a plane. I was terribly lucky to get these train tickets. Don't ask. Darling I don't know exactly where we're going. Spain first. South America if we can. Darling you're the one with the most Spanish. All those verbs you learned. I don't know what will happen to the rest of your clothes or your gadgets. Darling Grandma has decided she's staying here, she's feels she's too old for journeys and she'll just see what happens. Oh don't cry, darling. There... I need you to be strong. We all need to be strong.

Andrew what's the latest? Where's the fighting got to? Andrew turn it down for a second. Andrew talk to me.

Early stages

The ferns look happy, healthy
and green in the damp gloom.
The birches have grown strong stems
to rise to the light, above the roofs.

They must have craved nurture at the start.
And those acanthus will have needed
protection from the bully-boy slugs
till they got their footing.

Now they're established, fending for themselves.
Some input in the early years is all it takes,
till a root structure is in place, enough
to secure the nourishment surely there.

No-one would uproot plants,
turf them out of a pot they've filled
all their lives, and expect them
to survive alone in open ground.

These have settled in.
They have found the light,
those that seek it.
The others their shady corner.

Progress

First they let us live.
Then they let us do their jobs.
Then they let us live in their cities.
Then they let us live in their countryside.
Then they let us participate in their ceremonies.
Then they let us join their splendid army and police.
Then they let us feature in their advertising campaigns.
Then they let us direct their campaigns and plan their strategies.
Then they came for the weirdos, outsiders and extremists who were left,
who kept speaking out, refused to conform and clearly deserved it
and there were plenty of us to help
eliminate them.

'Be what you are'

Our school motto wasn't much used it's true,
and education should be about becoming,
not being, and not what you are but what you
could be, and perhaps it's a meaningless truism,
but still it's ironic that such a fluffy motto
was attached to a place where I was told
in no uncertain terms (the certain terms
were words I tried as badges on my blazer)
I could be myself once I'd left and not before,
thank you very much, you can do that kind
of thing at college, and it was ironic or significant
or something that I had to spend a tenner
on a poster saying 'It's alright to be you'
in big letters to pin up in my kitchen in my forties.

Spring

Finally you breeze in with a few daffs
and the promise things will be better,
suddenly flaunt a milder side,
release brief warmth, watch me uncurl
from cold hurt, still vulnerable,
then you snatch it back
behind the next cloud, in a cold snap,
now dangle hope again.
Is that supposed to make up for
keeping me in the dark
for months, on freeze,
putting me down,
locking me away,
going south for a laugh?
March was the end. As for April,
too many flowers now, too late.

Games

Fifteen on each side.
All in one spot if you're not careful.
With some poor lad at the bottom.
You have to keep an eye out.
There aren't normally accidents.
What's the harm in a few scratches?
It teaches competition.
Wheat from chaff.
Most boys love it.
The rest are poufs.
Probably prefer netball.
Best knock it out of them.

Anything up to thirty against one.
All the school if a name catches.
Some poor lad is the butt.
For a few weeks if a joke spreads.
Doesn't normally go on years.
Harmless fun mostly.
Toughens them up.
Very hard to stop it.
You can't have eyes everywhere.
Natural selection really.
Part of growing up.
Doesn't normally do lasting damage.

LEAVE

A shocking result,
so many marks on paper.
Who will clear up the mess?
Too late to claw back damage.

So many marks on paper.
Is there nothing you will miss?
Too late to claw back damage.
How can you leave yourself?

Is there nothing you will miss?
A handwritten note.
How can you leave yourself?
This will be a hard place to live in.

A handwritten note.
Who will clear up the mess?
This will be a hard place to live in.
A shocking result.

After me

my niece knows what she likes she likes
dogs Lego art carrots Minecraft
and now it's acrobatics too
my niece knows what she wants she wants
to do art with me we make
a paper picnic with plates she wants
to do Lego we make
a sea of blue white seethrough surging plastic bricks
my niece knows where to put each piece
in beautiful places connecting and contrasting
and surprising you should
see her cartwheels you should
see her trampoline leaps
my niece will be an artist after me

Tender

Here are swings, the chance to soar
for kids; alpines for the adults, stones
and slate, crunching underfoot,

and a yew, tall, dark, fastigiate,
a lone male without berries.

You head for the swings. At your age
you rarely step on playgrounds
and to step on tarmac which

bounces back, to find the ground
is cushioned, lifts you, like a smile,
boosts you, like love.

You store that warmth,
even if the spring sun
is undercut by chills.

Tender tarmac came too late for us,
but see, it need not have been hard.

The stones and slate will keep
these alpines warm and dry.

In the way

Painting the sky
on the walls won't work.
Make them go.
And outside
clouds are in the way
of the sky, banked up
back as far as I can reach,
stacked against the future,
too thick to see through,
too thin to climb,
dark on the underside,
the side they show.
Pack beasts,
they will not budge,
working with the wind
when it suits, though
they show each other
no solidarity. Nowhere
letting the light through.
Who would miss them?
'You will never really
be released, no let up.
We will never go away,'
they say, with the wind,
which never reverses,
will only turn, in time.
But beyond the towers
is a duck-blue hatch,
bright gap beneath
one far-flung cloud.
You have not given up.

In between

my bench on the hill,
the walk up,
the view down,
my sneaked half hour away

> my posters,
> on stained beige walls:
> Klee, Van Gogh;
> Bowie, Siouxsie

my books, by my bed:
Noel Streatfield, Judith Kerr;
Iris Murdoch, Edmund White

> my favourite jumper

long walks
on Sundays

conversations
with the bright teacher

> the trees from the window, homely forms
> those loving trees close up

moments alone with my first crush
limbs leaning in

art books borrowed
from the art room shelves

the first trendy outfit, black
and black; new respect

the art room after school;
music, choosing colours
mixed by me, placing shapes

the pub after life drawing;
two halves of bitter

the hug
the day we left:
the relief

the pub after everything

Keep calm and cross off

Once Crossrail has halved the Smoke,
bringing east and west to centre,
Topdownrail, or Upyoursrail, whateverrail
will quarter it, south to north.

Unfold that image, because then
they'll want Forwardslashrail,
the diagonal from Richmond to
Chigwell, through Islington.

They'll find it hard to resist completing
the map to make a nationalist logo,
and by this time flags and crowns
will be the country's main export,

(so many lines through the centre
they fuse, cool, and clear, the few
not riding through alighting to drink
where no-one thought to pause),

but resist they will.
Margins must be maintained.
Lines cannot be allowed to connect
only. They must also divide.

With the south-east corner torn
from our image along the folds,
or used for legends, adverts,
beneath which you still live,

Backslashrail will slide from Harrow down
through Hampstead to Centrepoint,
perhaps a little further, to the river,
but there it will stop.

Smudged

A hazard I swerve around,
rich brown, raspberry red, and nastier,
split against the filth
of the A2: an ex fox.

Next time I know to avoid it, a hump
contoured, drained of colour, merging
at the pace of London,
where death is average,
to conform with the asphalt,
flatter each day, squeegeed into Kent,
rolled like newsprint
up the West End and down
every shitty, oily street between.

There have been times
I've forgotten to look out,
ridden over the spot, spread it
on my narrow tyres.

It will be smudged
on the hallway floor,
where my bike rests,
all my floors,
my room where I lie flat.

Now I look for traces of it
on the road, see none,
see it everywhere.

Red and green make

Have you actually tried dividing
business from pleasure,
one e-mail for each, Sunday sacred,
computer off, phone silent,
no more than two drinks
with colleagues, no details,
definitely no flirting,
and never one of the last two
left in the pub at a conference?
Have you actually tried giving children
a rainbow of fresh Plasticine,
suggesting they make the things
each stripe implies, *green leaves,*
red tomato, yellow banana, blue eyes,
leaving them, to answer the phone,
check mail, expecting the colours
to stay in pure balls
ready to play with again
as their spectrum broadens,
green envy, red tie,
yellow brick road, blue bruise, but
returning to find them
on crayons now,
leaving behind what looks like
one big lump of *brown poo,*
striated, on inspection,
with every fluid hue possible,
entwined and mingled
deep inside each other,
no combination off limits,
inseparable and irreversible,
compromised and unworkable?

Three halves

Help yourselves, Alex says, places chocolate on the table and opens the wrapper, silver wings on all four sides. Three of them, at one end of the table. Charlie cracks a chunk free, one whole end of the bar at a jaunty angle, and eats it at face value, grinning both ways. Kim takes the lead from Charlie, now. No glance at Alex, now. Kim who made nothing clear, takes the other end, hadn't meant, perhaps, to break so much off. But now the bar is split again, up to Charlie's break. Kim's break veers away, leaving Alex a scant triangle, just one stretch of the straight edge. Kim halts, paralysed, staring at Charlie, who doesn't help. Kim eats it all, Kim who needed Alex' help at the start. Breaking the sliver in two, and handing one half to either side, Alex says, help yourselves.

You

I never got a Cistus through the winter;
our heavy soil, soggy sky. They like it light and dry.
Year on year, snow melt left salvia and rosemary
dead, fatsias blackened, brassicas rotten
in bitter rain, camellias burnt in the first sun.
I tried to see my garden through, to anticipate
cold shocks, cosseting with fleece,
cloches, mulch, considering drainage
and frost pockets, but by February left it,
beaten down. Talk of a year-round succession
of leaves and flowers, lamb's lettuce, hellebore,
escaped me. Other people's luck.
I emerged late spring to start from scratch,
re-sow.

I never got a relationship through the winter.
Sap retreated back to my stem,
foliage dropped from me, left a dark frame,
inert in the brief, low light as the temperature
fell to freezing. Flattened
under storms of impatience,
blizzards of mismatched expectation,
I flew south, returned to find myself
supplanted by a more vigorous specimen.
Yet this winter I have kept a succession
of fresh affection alive, kisses flowering
through the dark afternoons.
It's not that my cultivation has improved.
It's you.

FAQs of Gardens

Are they really in keeping,
these foreign plants,
palms and tree ferns?

You're not asking us
to dig them up
now their roots are in deep,
now they're intertwined?
Do you think belonging
means sameness?
Who says what fits where?
Get with the new ecology.

Do they really like it here?

You can't see them,
sprouting and blooming,
fronds frolicking
through the flat-leaved trees?
Contributing carbon
for all they're worth?

Can we provide for
their cultural needs?

These plants
will sort themselves out.
They have the conditions
they need.
Can you provide for yours?
Do you even know
what they are?

Dasylirion? Have I said
the name right?

No. Make an effort.
You can say dandelion alright.

Were they sown round here?

A lot of them, yes.
Some in Holland.
Some in the opposite hemisphere.
Does it matter?

What do you mean it was
all just swamps here once?

Why do you think
the streets have names
like Lower Marsh?
It was bogs from here
to Croydon,
no Victorian terraces,
or London planes,
which are the hybrid offspring
of immigrants, by the way.

Aren't they taking over?

So what if they are?
Deal with it.

Is there any space left?

Yes.

Snails

deserve sympathy, and glowing odes,
the way tanks do. Consider smallpox.
Tanks were modelled on them, also bulldozers,
and Daleks. They echo the creeping low
brought on by rain. They live off my misery.
Their steady menace is Iago's, Stalin's,
closer to home the approach of the
top dog and his heavies down a corridor.
People are shocked at what I do to them,
what any gardener does, crunch them under foot,
bisect with secateurs, squash them in my fingers,
throw rocks, hold flowers in their path, chant, yell,
paint banners, load slingshots,
and get back on with life as best I can.

Clematis has the last laugh

Finding light is a race to the top.
Height helps,
and best keep thin.
As a climber
I know that, and
mock the jostling trees
as they compete.
I breach discrete species,
linking individualist limbs
like it or not, forcing
upwardly mobile birches
and stolid beeches
to join hands like
a luvved-up party guest,
weaving my way
through the boughs
flirting and stirring it,
unchecked,
leaving trouble behind
and rising above
to lounge on the canopy
and open my flowers
in broad daylight.

About Steph Morris

Steph Morris is an artist, gardener, writer and translator. He grew up in the midlands, lived in Berlin for many years and is now based in London. His poems have been published in various magazines and in anthologies including *Diversifly*, also from Fair Acre Press. In 2019 he won the Live Canon 'Borough Prize'. His translations include novels by Martin Suter, the diaries of Brigitte Reimann, forthcoming from Seagull, several books about Pina Bausch and work for the Pina Bausch Foundation. His poetry translations have appeared in *MPT* and on no-mans-land.org, including work by Kurt Drawert and Tina Stroheker. He is currently translating Isa Aichinger's poetry and dialogues. He graduated from the Poetry School / Newcastle University MA in Writing Poetry in 2017 as part of the inaugural cohort.

steph-morris.com

@herr_morris on twitter

Acknowledgements

'What to take on flight' was first published in *Rialto*. 'Early stages' and 'Three halves' appeared on *Ink Sweat & Tears*. 'Clematis has the last laugh', 'FAQs of Gardens' and other 'Early stages' were planted on Bonnington Square as part of the Poetry School's Mixed Borders scheme in 2016. 'FAQs of gardens' was first published in the anthology *Write to be counted*. 'Keep calm and cross off' was displayed as part of Mixed Borders 2017 in the House of St Barnabas garden. It won the 2019 Live Canon 'Borough Prize'. It was first published in the *2019 Live Canon Anthology*. 'Snails' appeared in *Ambit 241*.

The title of this pamphlet is from a sign photographed in a flowerbed in Waterloo, London, outside the Festival Hall in 2017. Thanks to the gardener/poet. Please come forward; we were unable to trace you.

Thanks to all to my poetry tutors, fellow students and poet peers for their nurture, and the poetry publishers and organisers for the spade-work. I have found the poetry scene friendly. Thank you all. Particular thanks to my MA cohort, to Tamar Yoseloff, Jacqueline Saphra, Nadia Kingsley, Dan Musset, Miranda Peake, and the Greenwich poets.